MOTHER WIT

FOR THE

BUSINESS WOMAN

*What Your Momma Couldn't Tell You
and Your Daddy Never Did*

By

ICY D GINES

ISBN 1-58597-265-7

Library of Congress Control Number: 2004092860

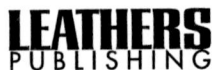

A division of Squire Publishers, Inc.
4500 College Blvd.
Leawood, KS 66211
1/888/888-7696
www.leatherspublishing.com

Dedication

In loving memory of my dear mother, Irene Frison Hyde, who showed me instead of telling me, took me instead of sending me, led me instead of pushing me, and guided me instead of driving me;

and

To my daughters, Alinda J. and Joan H., who live by mother wit and are surviving the workplace, and who encouraged me to write this book to help other women meet their highest potential and desires.

TABLE OF CONTENTS

WHAT YOUR MOMMA COULDN'T TELL YOU AND YOUR DADDY NEVER DID

Whether slow evolution or lack of revolution, people at work do not respond well to a touchy-feely approach. Simple instructions that are strictly enforced get better results than meaningful dialogue.

By the time I figured this out, my mother had already learned it the hard way. As a first-generation business woman, she travailed in the workplace in the 1960s as my sister and I watched reruns of *Leave It To Beaver.* Then, in the 1970s, she struggled to advance while my sister and I thought nothing of Mary Tyler Moore's preference of career over domesticity. By the 1980s and 1990s, my mother had a great store of knowledge that my sister and I could forage as we fought to establish our places in the working world as second-generation business women.

The first job I remember Momma having was billing clerk for a meat company. After that, she worked as a clerk in a large government agency, where she advanced to top-level management. She retired with 28 years of soft skills at her command, and she saw and experienced the entire gamut of office politics and management styles. In her book, *God Don't Make Oops!,* Momma shared the difficulties, discouragement and delusions she experienced as employee and manager.

Momma never pushed us or gave us advice about our careers unless we asked for it. When we did ask, she could recall times when she experienced similar situations and bring them forward for our guidance.

The things that she endured and suffered left her with a plethora of wisdom that she not only shares with us, but with anyone who asks. However, our worlds are small compared to the large workforce of women that may be struggling with common business issues for the first time or may benefit from reinforcement of sometimes cold business principles administered with the gentle warmth of a mother guiding her daughters.

Momma's wisdom has gotten us through our most difficult situations and times of workplace distress. Following her advice, you will weather many problems and avoid many more.

If you relish office politics and enjoy becoming embroiled in all manner of water-cooler controversy, this book is not for you. If you didn't know you shouldn't wear "hoochie" clothes to work or pop gum in the office, consider first obtaining a basic etiquette manual. But, if you want to find the most effective and direct way to accomplish your career goals with the least amount of emotional stress, read on.

For quick reference, this book is divided into a list of major lessons that Momma taught us. Each chapter contains a short discussion on how the lesson may be applied.

The chapter rules are instructions handed down from mother to daughter, sometimes by way of grandmother, though some of the quotes are in the public domain.

— The daughters of Icy D Gines

CHAPTER 1

SMILE

Rule: A pleasant smile is one of your most valuable assets. For a successful business woman, being able to smile in any situation is a grace. Some people even consider smiling and a cheerful countenance a duty. Smiling will smooth your way in job interviews and in any circumstances requiring strength of character.

Some people learn the usefulness of smiling at a very young age, but to others it is an acquired skill. When one of my daughters was a teenager, she never smiled. She thought it wasn't sophisticated to smile and that being expected to smile was a violation of her personal liberties and individuality.

Then, she flunked her driver's test and, in tears, wondered why. She thought that as long as she knew what she was doing, her attitude didn't matter. But, oh, how she wanted to drive!

I told her, "Honey, you've got to learn to smile."

She wondered what her smile had to do with anything and, seeing her confusion, I pushed her up to a mirror and said, "Stand in front of this mirror and learn to make a pretty smile that doesn't seem forced. Then practice changing your expression to a smile when you feel yourself with any other expression."

In two to three weeks, she took her driver's test again. She walked into the license bureau smiling and smiled walking out with her driver's license.

She hadn't learned any new driving skills. Instead, she had learned a skill that would be invaluable throughout her life.

Now, let me say that I know some women will consider this advice to cultivate a nice smile condescending and reflective of a sexist culture. Only defeatists fear that cultivating a smile is sexist. My daughters have told me that in their travels they've noticed that the profes-

1

sionals that they most admire, male and female, have attractive smiles. The most charming, powerful and influential individuals have the ability to smile in the most awkward or infuriating circumstances, and their "pretty" smiles are a badge of their courage and self control.

When I began my career, I noticed that the majority of my co-workers looked worried, anxious, mean or just, plain unhappy. They rarely smiled and were very unfriendly.

I started smiling when I was told that I couldn't have a position that I knew I could do and was well qualified for. They gave me no specific reason for refusing me the job. My smile completely startled them.

Seeing their reaction to my smile made me wonder whether I had intimidated them by smiling at their rejection. Noting their reaction, I decided to make smiling habitual. I knew that some people would consider me a push-over, but they would also be surprised by how effectively cutting words were delivered with a smile.

At one point, I had a mentor and friend who advised me never to lose my smile. It has not always been easy.

Once when our office called a meeting of managers, things got pretty ugly because I was accused of falsifying documents. I excused myself from the meeting to get the evidence to verify my information. When I returned with the proof, the air went out of my accusers' sails.

I had smiled the entire time I was being accused and smiled as I produced my proof.

As I walked down the hall after the meeting, one of my peers told me, "I would have been furious if they accused me of falsifying records. But you just smiled. I don't understand you. I don't know whether you know something that nobody else knows or if you are just stupid."

I gave her my biggest, prettiest smile and said, "You are supposed to be the intelligent one. You decide." Then I quickened my steps, leaving her staring at my back. She didn't know that I was burning to vindicate myself against my accusers. But what would that have accomplished?

Smiling will allow you to do and say things that would otherwise be unacceptable. For example, once, when an officer in my company was in an exceptionally foul mood, we passed in the hall and I smiled at him. When he did not return my smile, I said, "What's wrong today? Did you take two nasty pills instead of the one?"

He stopped abruptly, and I rushed by him. Within ten minutes my manager called me into his office and asked me what had I said to the officer. The officer had called my manager and asked him to talk to me. The officer said that I had stuck a knife in his back and smiled as I turned the handle, but that he could say nothing because I smiled the entire time.

My manager told me to be less frank, which was wise advice. However, if I had not smiled, I would have been seriously reprimanded.

People can tell if your smile is genuine. Remember that a phony smile indicates deception, but a genuine smile can disarm the worst critic.

A word of caution: know your audience when you use your charming smile to accomplish something that would otherwise fetch a "No." Smiling at the wrong time can backfire on you.

When is the wrong time to smile? It is inadvisable to smile in highly tense situations. At one meeting, I knew that my manager was in a very foul mood as I walked into his office. He was yelling at one of my peers about a problem caused by information he had given her. All of the other staffers had their heads down when I walked into the office.

My first mistake was being late. So, in my eagerness to make up for it, I said, "Hello, isn't it a nice day?"

He turned to me and said, "First, you come in late, and then you have the nerve to disturb my meeting. Don't you see that it isn't a 'nice day' for some of us? What are you trying to do, make me look bad?" Not only should I have been on time for the meeting, but I should have quietly entered the room and taken my seat with my eyes down.

Take care that your smile is not condescending. I had a difficult manager who had caused me major problems on the job and tarnished my otherwise good reputation with upper management. We were locked in a battle of wills.

However, he was new to his job and made numerous technical mistakes. Knowing that it was uncharitable of me, I gave him intentionally condescending smiles whenever I saw that he was having problems. He recognized what I was doing, and my evaluations plummeted.

Eventually he was transferred, but he left a scar on my employment record that took long, hard work to repair. Thinking back, regardless of his actions, it was probably my own fault.

— CHAPTER 2 —

TONE IS EVERYTHING

Rule: *Voice tone can be a powerful weapon. Use it to your advantage. Often, it's not what you say, but how you say it.*

As in musical notes, there are various octaves of speech. A voice may be high, low or bass, and some people speak in hard-to-understand monotones.

Tone is one of the things in your life that you can control. Unlike most genetic traits, most people can temper their voice and tone. An overly high voice, which people may not take seriously, with practice, may be moderated. You can learn to speak softly and make your soft voice travel.

Even a baby responds to the tone of a voice. A harsh voice will cause her to cry, while a gentle voice will dry tears and calm her.

An animal responds to tones, too. For example, if you offer a steak to your dog, while saying with a harsh voice, "Here is your steak, come and get it," the dog will fear drawing near, even for a juicy steak. But if you call the dog in a calm, sweet voice, it will not only come immediately, but it may lick you or wag its tail, even without your offering a steak.

Some people think that a loud voice is most likely to command attention. However, try talking with an interested tone, but in a barely audible voice. People will usually give you their undivided attention and strain to hear what you are saying.

Regardless of how captivating your subject may be, no one will listen if you talk about it in a monotone. Ask someone whose voice you admire to teach you not to speak in monotone.

One of my managers spoke in monotone. Every sentence he spoke sounded like a continuance from a previous sentence. In meetings, half of the staff nodded while others passed notes or doodled.

Your voice should complement what you say, and explain what you mean. Try saying the following statement in three different tones, "Did you hear me calling you?" Now say it again and imagine that you are the person being addressed. Which tone made you angry or disinterested and which tone got your attention?

Say, "What did you say?" in several different tones and decide which one is most irritating or which makes you angry.

As an aside, some people talk just for the heck of it; others talk because they like to hear their own voice, and still others talk to impress. Momma used to say, "Don't talk just to hear your head rattle." And quoted the Bible, "A fool's voice is known by his multitude of words" *(Ecclesiastes 6: 3b)*. Talking too much can get you into trouble. It is wise to think before you speak. When you do talk, remember that tone is everything.

Your tone can command attention or cause anger, admiration or distrust. The way you say "hello" to your manager or co-workers displays your attitude and gives an impression, real or false, about how you feel or what you are thinking. Nothing is more insulting or turns people off faster than someone speaking in a perpetual growl. Remember, tone is everything!

— CHAPTER 3 —

SET A GOOD EXAMPLE

Rule: *Good examples are few and far between. Set one.*

We live in an age when everybody wants to do what they want regardless of what the rules are, how it looks on their records or how others, even their employer, regard them.

Some people may think that setting a good example means being an apple polisher. But being a good example means doing what is right just because it is right. It also means doing and saying what you would not be ashamed for someone to mimic.

If you want to be the first one considered for that promotion, then you should consider your actions and how your manager views your work habits. It doesn't matter what your co-workers think: it's what your employer thinks that matters. Here are some ways to be a good example in your workplace:

Being a good employee starts with being on time for work. Employees who are always late for work show how little they care for their jobs and respect their boss, even when they plan to stay late to make up lost time. Working hours are purposefully established, and you are being paid to observe those times.

Absolutely nothing is as refreshing as an employee with a good attitude. It is not always easy, but if you are consistent in your attitude, others will know at all times where you stand and appreciate it.

Be known for your honesty and forthrightness. Don't play games. Games are not only childish, but they show your immaturity and unwillingness to accept responsibility. Say what you mean and mean what you say. Act without hidden motives, because when hidden motives surface, you will be thought of as a manipulator.

Always be willing to admit when you have made a mistake. Take responsibility for your actions, and don't blame others to get yourself off the hook.

Know when to share. Everything is not for sharing. When your employer tells you something in confidence, if you share what you know and it gets back to the wrong source, it could cause problems. When you are training others, tell them the basics and only what they need to know to accomplish their work. Telling them more can confuse them. Let them rely on you if they need more information. Knowledge really is power.

It is good to learn from your own mistakes, but it is wiser to learn from the mistakes of others. There's an old saying that goes, "Anybody can profit from his own mistakes, but a wise man profits from another's mistakes," that is what I mean.

Watch out for cliques, because they can cause you much distress. What is a clique? It is a tightly knit group of people that gossip about everything and everybody and usually tries to control all of the activities of a department or organization. The group is hard to penetrate and, when you do, it is almost impossible to get out of. It is run by a bunch of people who think that they are the best thing since sliced bread and they hold each other in the highest esteem. Non-members are considered the scum of the earth and are not welcome and are personas non grata.

There was a clique in the agency where I worked. These three ladies were from different parts of the agency but were considered the best and smartest in the organization. They were brought in to establish a new system for processing documents. When meetings were held, they were the focus of all conversation. When others asked a question or had comments, the three "Wonder Women," as they were called, either ignored or ridiculed them.

Another manager wanted to be accepted by them and tried to break into the clique. After doing everything in her power to gain acceptance, including agreeing with everything they said, trailing them around and suffering stinging insults, she was somewhat accepted. Eventually, the wonder women were transferred to other areas, leaving her behind. Although she tried to be friends with the remaining managers, nobody wanted to be friends with her anymore because of her behavior when she was trying to be part of the clique.

Know when to be flexible. If you are too flexible, you will be labeled wishy-washy, or unable to make a firm decision. But if you are inflexible, you will get the reputation of being stubborn and uncooperative.

All of us are sometimes tempted to tell the big fish story about the one that got away, but **avoid the temptation to exaggerate** because when the facts are found out, you may be labeled a liar. Once that happens, it is most difficult, if not impossible, to shake the label.

Don't expect all employers to be fair and objective. But being treated unfairly should not keep you from setting a good example. In the end, you will be respected and given opportunities that others are not given because of your tenacity and trustworthiness. Who knows but that you will inspire others to imitation?

— CHAPTER 4 —

BE READY TO WORK TWICE AS HARD

Rule: *Nobody owes you anything but a chance. It is your job to take the chance you are given and show the stuff you are made of.*

Do your job better than anybody else could. Go that extra mile.

Never refuse an assignment, even if you don't know what it entails. Be available for any special assignment, especially if it has a high profile. Often, a project that no one else wants ends up being the best pick.

Don't let others keep you from shining. If you are part of a project with others, pay close attention to deadlines and do everything in your power not to miss the deadline. If the deadline is eminent and you have completed your part but others haven't, send an e-mail to the project leader informing him/her that your portion is complete and offering to help others if necessary. Be sure to copy the e-mail to your manager and everyone involved in the project. But be prepared to get hostile return e-mail or even a visit from those who are not keeping up their end of the project. If you have kept the project manager informed, little can be said. This kind of documentation will prevent anyone from accusing you of being the one holding up the project. Keep your project leader and your manager informed and show your willingness to help others and be a team player.

Be willing to take on every job that you are given without complaining or boasting. This will enhance your reputation as a hard worker.

Don't be surprised when your supervisor gives you twice as much to do as anyone else. She is trying to see just how far you can be pushed before saying, "Wait a minute! Don't you see that I already have an impossible workload? I can't do this." Never give her that satisfaction.

Never complain about your workload. Once, I made that mistake, and my manager told me that because he didn't see my eyes crossed, I was not overworked. Then the pressure was really on!

When my workload was especially heavy, the solution for managing my workload was setting priorities. Few people can successfully work multiple projects at once and meet all of their deadlines without effective time management. *(See Chapter 9 on "Free Your Mind and the Rest Will Follow")*. There may even come a time when you should ask your manager to help you set priorities. In most cases, she will be happy to assist you and knows that you have need of her involvement.

If you are unfortunate enough to report to several levels of management, you should identify chains of command. Nothing makes a manager more angry than feeling that you have ignored him by skipping to another level of management which, in most cases, is his immediate boss.

Unless otherwise advised by your direct manager, priority should always be given to the highest level of management's request. Then, work down the chain of command to your direct manager. Again, if there is a conflict in needs or requests, ask your immediate manager for help in prioritizing. This will show him that you respect his authority and want his positive involvement.

If your direct manager has an urgent need and you also have an urgent request from upper management that your manager may be unaware of, send e-mail to your manager with a copy to upper management explaining your situation, but by no means complain. This will require them to come together and decide your priorities. Take care not to use words or statements that might seem accusative or insensitive to either party.

This will also prevent stress build-up from trying to accomplish both projects or making a decision, which might not be appropriate for you to make. It is very difficult to perform efficiently under stress, so eliminate it as much as possible.

If possible, always be at work before your boss. If that's not possible, at least be there before your boss gets there sometimes. That is not always easy, but it will pay off in the long run.

In any event, never call your boss to explain your tardiness with a poor excuse. You don't have a baby sitter, the car won't start, and you overslept are invalid excuses. Even if your excuse is valid, don't use it as a reason for habitual tardiness. Being late constantly indicates that your job is not important to you and shows disrespect for your manager and co-workers.

Nothing impresses your manager more than your taking initiative on projects or originating ideas that will benefit the organization, especially if you carry them through. Hint: if you are sure that your idea is a good one but not sure that your manager will allow you to do it, go ahead and do it without asking. Sometimes it is better to apologize later than ask permission before. Only, **be positive** that your actions are good for the company and will not backfire on you. You may come out smelling like a rose!

Managers look for people they can depend on to be team players. Don't be selfish, or you will be branded as a know-it-all or back-stabber. Others may have ideas as good as yours. You will be greatly rewarded and will rise in the eyes of your employer and peers if you are willing to cooperate with others.

— CHAPTER 5 —

DON'T TAKE IT PERSONALLY, EVEN IF IT IS

Rule: It is inevitable that you will encounter people who just don't like you, during your career. Some people take pride in making others miserable, but don't take it personally, even if it is meant to be personal.

There are people who were raised in a miserable environment and just don't understand anything else. Causing others hurt or discomfort seems to be their badge of honor. They take no interest in creating an atmosphere that is conducive to good relationships and may even feel threatened when everybody seems to get along. There are others who take personal baggage with them everywhere they go. When confronted with these kinds of people, do everything in your power to stay focused on the work instead of on them.

I once had a manager who made my life miserable without meaning to. She was a workaholic and expected everybody else to be. She pushed us to our limits and still expected more. She was particularly fond of pushing me and called me into her office every day at 4:15 p.m., knowing that quitting time was 4:30 p.m. I would not be dismissed until after 5 p.m. It would not have been so bad if she did not have the mouth of a sailor. Every other word was profanity, and seeing my distaste for her choice words seemed to energize her. This was the least of my troubles with her.

I was very relieved and happy when she transferred to another department. But shortly after her transfer, one of her new employees came to me in tears and told me that she worked and talked to them like they were her slaves. I told her that she had done the same to us and that it was just her way. Then I realized that I shouldn't have taken her behavior as personally as I had. She treated me no differently than she treated others.

In another case, I had a manager who actually did have a personal dislike for me. When we got a new manager, we all looked forward to working with her, hoping that she would not be as hard on us. The day she breezed in with an expensive piece of art tucked under her arm, we were all impressed. Little did we know that she would be ten times worse that our last manager.

Unfortunately, she made me one of her favorites. Those she did not select became her enemies for no apparent reason. However, anyone not agreeing with her quickly fell out of favor. She also expected you to discuss your personal life with her.

I championed her cause, but drew the line where talking about my private life was concerned. Thus, I soon found myself exiled. This was not unusual because it seemed that every few months there was a shuffle of who was in and who was out.

I was now "out," and her suspicion and dislike for me were personal.

In some cases, you will never know if someone's treatment of you is personal. Regardless, your objective must be to not allow it to affect your performance negatively.

My daughter, who is an attorney, must regularly appear before a judge who is berating and condescending.

Early in her career she was subjected to thinly veiled, sexist remarks usually directed toward her clients, and outright hostility often directed at her. She routinely sought my counsel before appearing before him.

One day she told me that the one advantage of having to appear before this judge was that it made her a better lawyer. She had to be doubly well prepared when appearing before him in anticipation of his questioning her competence if she slipped in the least.

It wasn't his intention, but his abrasive manner had the indirect effect of making her a better lawyer. Still, the anxiety she felt in merely anticipating confrontation with him was costing her sleep and confidence.

This went on for years until one morning I heard her mention to her associate attorney that she didn't seem to be as disturbed when she had to appear before this judge. Her associate responded that it was always unpleasant, but she didn't take it personally.

This let me know two things: First, this judge was probably rude to everyone at one time or another (which turned out to be true), and second, my daughter had completely personalized his demeanor as a reflection on her, when some, if not all, of it probably wasn't.

I took my daughter aside and gently but firmly told her, "Honey, being insulting and nasty is who he is. Just smile when he is being ugly and say under your breath, "You are a jerk, always will be a jerk, so why should I think you will change?"

When you are picked out to be picked on, ask yourself why. It could be for any number of reasons or for no reason at all.

If you can't figure out why, discreetly talk to a co-worker, but remember that the truth may hurt. Be prepared for the worst, including being told that you are your own worst enemy. If you are not willing to hear criticism, or if you are overly sensitive, do not ask others, even your best friends, for their opinion.

Learning not to take things that happen or that are said to you personally will improve how you deal with others. You will gain a sense of freedom as you realize that you don't have to hold yourself accountable for other's behavior. Check yourself, and then consider the source.

— CHAPTER 6 —

MAKE YOURSELF INDISPENSABLE

Rule: They say "one monkey don't stop no show." But, if you want to be the first promoted and the last in the unemployment line, make yourself indispensable.

Being indispensable does not mean being constantly in the boss's office or in her face. It does mean that you perform your job at the highest quality level and constantly add to your skills.

Be the first on the cutting edge of technology and introducing ideas that will result in a more efficient and effective operation. This means reading. Read about your industry and sidelines related to your industry and job. One easy way to do this is subscribing to Interest News Services, specially those that will notify you as issues come up in your area of interest.

Think of ways to present your ideas and department procedures using charts and graphs or develop simple statistics that may show cost savings to the company. Develop ways to help your employer compile numbers or referral sources that will quickly show how well a department is functioning. In doing this, make sure you look at the big picture and ensure data accuracy, because jobs could be affected and your reputation is at stake. Don't be offended if your proposal is defeated. It may take a while to develop a reputation for ingenuity.

Faithfulness on your job may make you indispensable. If you can be relied upon to be at your desk when needed or relied upon to know all of the specifics about your job, your co-workers and boss will get into the habit of coming to you as the "expert."

— CHAPTER 7 —

IF YOU LEARN THE LINGO, YOU'LL WRITE TO PLEASE

Rule: Writing is a major part of any career. You must master the written word if you want to succeed and avoid embarrassment.

Letter writing was my weak spot and the problem area that gave me the greatest heartburn in my career. I was never good at writing and my grammar was awful. I learned writing skills the hard way, and here is what I learned.

(1) You must know for whom your communication is intended and your subject matter. These things will tell you how to present your document. You may know all of the details about a subject, but if your supervisor does not understand the details it will not be acceptable. Write in a way that your audience understands the information being presented.

New on the job, my manager assigned me to respond to a memorandum. As he didn't give me specific instructions, I researched and gathered all of the information pertaining to the subject. I was proud of my finished product and placed it in a folder on his desk.

The next morning, the folder was on my desk, and when I opened it I was hurt to see ugly red marks all over my beautifully-written memorandum. I asked my manager what was wrong with the memorandum. I told him that I had researched all of the information and knew that it was accurate, but he said, "This is one of the worst memorandums I have ever seen."

He did not tell me what was wrong with the memorandum or tell me what he was looking for. But I restructured the memorandum and again placed it on his desk.

The next day, the memorandum was again back on my desk with

ugly red marks, but the marks did not tell me what was wrong.

Frustrated, I went into his office and put the memorandum, not too gently, on his desk, and told him that the facts were accurate. I also said that I did not understand what he wanted, and walked away. He rewrote my memorandum.

The following day, I asked my manager's secretary if he had given her the rewritten memorandum, and she said that he had. I asked for a copy.

After reading the memorandum, I understood what he was looking for. The information was the same, but it was embellished by adding words that elaborated the facts, played the political game, and used words that were so big that I had to get a dictionary to find their meaning. The memo was clearly meant to impress the reader. I discovered later that he was writing to a high-level audience while I had been writing to a different audience.

I then went to the office files and read other memorandums he had written. I learned that, regardless of how accurate your work is, if it is not written for the right audience, it is not adequate. I learned to write like my manager, which often required using the dictionary and thesaurus.

(2) It is imperative that your tone is appropriate. Like your verbal communication, your written communication carries tone. Consider this statement: "Your letter inferred that we were negligent in addressing your issue." The tone in this sentence is hostile and will draw an angry response. A much better statement would be, "We received your letter and are sorry that we did not supply the information you needed. However, if you would give us the type of information you are looking for, we will make every effort to comply with your request." In the latter sentence, even if the customer was in error, the tone and gentle touch will cause the customer to take another look at his or her request. More importantly, you will maintain the business relationship.

(3) Make sure you understand the phrases and acronyms unique to the companies, and use them correctly. Also, if you can, repeat the recipient's words or catch-phrases when addressing that person. Try to be sure that everyone is talking the same language. Don't be reluctant to ask the meaning of an acronym if you don't understand it.

(4) Knowing the lingo also means using proper protocol. Be sure that appropriate sign-offs and initials are on file and that you have

copies of all of your correspondence to prove that all affected parties saw it. If you are responding to a controversial issue, you should keep a copy of the correspondence for your personal file as well in case you are called upon to prove or disprove an allegation or if an issue arises during your yearly evaluation.

All of the above apply to e-mail, too. Except with e-mail, there is also a tendency to be too casual. Avoid casual e-mail and remember never to write anything in e-mail that you would hate to see posted on the office bulletin board.

Be up-front and open with your supervisor or peers in your memos and e-mail. Ask for your supervisor's feedback on your writing even if it makes him squirm and makes you uncomfortable. It will pay off in the long run. Don't forget when you get the feedback that sometimes it may be necessary to take copious notes to refer back to.

— CHAPTER 8 —

PLAY WITH A PUPPY
AND IT WILL LICK YOUR MOUTH

Rule: The proverb, "familiarity breeds contempt," means that culti-vating a very personal relationship with co-workers may result in their disrespect or scorn because you have made yourself "common." My mother put it this way: "Play with a puppy and it will lick your mouth; play with a child and it will sass you out!"

I grew up on a farm. Even though dogs were our pets, they were considered animals and stayed outdoors. They ran free on the farm, caught most of their food and would eat almost anything. Since we did not know where they had been or what they had eaten, we considered letting them lick our faces unsanitary.

We had a puppy named Spot. I loved the puppy and played with him all of the time, but I did not like him licking my face. As I was playing with him one day, he licked my face before I could stop him. He knew that I would not like it, but he also knew that he could get away with it. I had become too familiar with the dog and had not trained him not to lick my face.

So it is with people; they will go as far as you let them. If you let them go too far, sooner or later you will be embarrassed or angry at what they say or how they treat you in public.

One of my female co-workers had been too friendly with a male peer. We were all out to lunch one day when he playfully patted her on her behind. She was angry and upset, partly because she knew that we all saw him do it, but she could say nothing to the man because most of us had seen him touch her before and she had ignored it. Their relationship invited it.

Now, I am not talking about sexual harassment. I am talking about a woman who may allow what she thinks is just a playful gesture, in private, will ultimately embarrass her in public if she lets it continue.

In another instance, my manager loved to tell others her personal business. It didn't seem to matter who it was. She didn't understand that there are things that you don't discuss, especially with your employees. She also expected everyone to share their personal affairs with her and became angry when they would not do so. Everybody knew the type of person she was, because she had told everybody her most intimate actions and they were not pretty. When stink gets on you, it's hard to wash off.

Then one day it all came home to roost. When my manager left the agency, the stink followed her and she was in the worst possible position. Although she was new to the organization, everybody knew her personal affairs. It's difficult enough for a supervisor to consistently maintain the respect of her staff without sabotaging herself with her past.

Please keep in mind that you are in your place of employ to do a job, not to be popular, or to win friends and influence people. It is not necessary to be friends to work well with someone.

I don't mean that you should not be friendly, but becoming personal friends with managers and co-workers can cause problems. It is best to avoid detailed discussions with your co-workers about your family, intimate personal life, and deepest, darkest, secrets. It is never a good idea to indulge in gossip about other employees. When you are no longer friends with your confidantes, your entire life will be the subject of gossip and the employees you talked about will hate you.

In another case, a lady I know is self-employed in a small office. She relied heavily on her staff to perform their duties and also as a social outlet, taking them to dinner after work and even dressing up with them on Halloween.

However, when employment issues arose and it was time to correct an employee, she was surprised and hurt that the employee's response was always emotional and volatile. She also couldn't understand why they wouldn't work especially hard for her since she had been a friend to them. As for the employees, they couldn't understand the woman's shifts back and forth between friend and employer . The results was resentment.

The bottom line is that all people need emotional and social boundaries, and you need to purposely set boundaries with your managers and co-workers. Crossing those boundaries makes for confusion and even anger. It is very difficult to repair a working relationship that's had its personal boundaries broken without resulting casualties.

— CHAPTER 9 —

FREE YOUR MIND
AND THE REST WILL FOLLOW

Rule: *Hard work never killed anyone … but stress has.*

Between family, church and other activities, pressure is high. There is no magic formula for stress. Like some types of medicine, what might be a cure for one can be fatal to another. You know your own personality better than anyone, so be yourself and work with what you have.

Find your own way to handle stress, whether it be confrontation, withdrawal, or taking work home with you. Don't be afraid to work late or at home if it will take some of the stress off and make it easier in the office during your normal work hours.

Late in my career, I learned the danger of stress. One of my managers relied on me to do all of her responsibilities, even to the point of preparing my own and her evaluations. Because I was not accustomed to taking work home, I tried to complete my job and hers, with all of the stress of the office around me.

After a while, I started getting hives and severe headaches. Each morning, I dreaded reporting to work to the point that severe cramps doubled me over when I pulled into the parking lot.

Then I awoke one morning, but could not get out of bed because of severe vertigo. Everything spun around, even when my eyes were closed. At the hospital, I was diagnosed with a brain-stem stroke.

I knew that my problem was stress and that I had to do something about it to live. So I started staying overtime and "hiding" in a spare office when there was a time crunch.

However, I made no progress in managing my workload, and it seemed that the harder I worked, the further I got behind. I didn't know what to do, and my manager didn't seem to notice or care about my dilemma. I knew not to complain about my workload and that it was my responsibility to develop a plan to manage my workload while reducing stress.

The questions rattling around in my head were, "What should I do first, what had priority?" I had notes here, torn paper there and scribbles everywhere, even in my purse and on my desk, on the computer, on the file cabinet, on the door, on the kitchen table, on the refrigerator ... The few things that I had not written somewhere I made the mistake of trying to remember.

With all these things haunting you, it's easy to become disgruntled and just plain hard to get along with. You suffer, your family suffers, and the people you work with wish you had stayed at home.

I started setting priorities, developing task lists and delegating authority. This helped organize my workload and manage stress.

The solution for managing my workload was setting priorities. Few people can successfully work multiple projects at once and meet all of their deadlines without effective time management. There may even come a time when you should ask your manager to help you set deadlines. In most cases, she will be happy to assist you, knowing that you have need of her involvement.

Learning time management skills will prove invaluable. When the agency said that we were to go to a session on time management, I thought, "I don't have time to go; I can manage my time," but I had no choice.

Attending that class was the best thing that could happen for my career. Learning to plan my time freed up my mind, because I found that I didn't have to remember everything. Using a planner to store and prioritize my numerous notes and pieces of paper, I was able to keep track of events, dates and times.

Suddenly, my overwhelming workload was manageable. I no longer had to come in early and work late. I no longer took work home with me.

In fact, I was amazed at how effective the planner was. I felt as though a load had been lifted from my mind. My mind was a bird freed from its cage. Now I could relax and be free from worry about remembering deadlines and meetings. Within a week, my insomnia left and the migraines were dramatically reduced. My attitude improved, too.

Every morning I used my planner to decide which tasks I would complete and their order, rearranging them daily to track my workload. I carried my planner in my purse, and it went everywhere with me. It gave me confidence.

If you are one of those people who feel you do not need to plan, you will have problems unless you teach yourself to juggle and throw several projects, meetings, ideas and goals in the air, while knowing exactly where and when they will land.

Please understand, having extolled the virtues of using a written planner to prioritize, you must still learn the art of multi-tasking. Most women will learn this from watching their mothers. I learned watching mine. Apply this skill to your job duties.

It was not by deliberate demonstrations that my mother taught me to multi-task, but by simply watching her elegantly manage the domestic demands of a large, agrarian family. Her kitchen was my classroom. She would light the fire in the wood-burning iron stove to boil water, knead bread dough that she had prepared the night before, flour chicken while keeping an eye on the boiling water, and run water to wash the green beans in one pan and her bowls and utensils in a second pan, all perfectly timed and choreographed so that the meal-making ended as we all sat to say grace.

Much later, I realized that I had learned the skill of doing several things at once and bringing them all to successful conclusion from my mother. This proved to be an asset to my career. My daughters have commented on the advantage of learning multi-tasking from their mother, too.

I believe that it is possible for young women who didn't have the advantage of watching an industrious mother, to gain multi-tasking skills of necessity. If you lack these skills or need to develop them, start by practicing doing one thing that you consider easy or do well, and then add another thing that you can do simultaneously. Then gradually add tasks to your litany just as an amateur juggler adds balls to her routine. A time will come, however, when even multi-tasking skill gives way to overload and using a written planner is critical.

CHAPTER 10

NEVER GO AFTER
THE PROTECTED ONE

Rule: *Avoid criticizing or discussing the protected person, because his or her sponsor will take it as a direct assault. This includes "constructive criticism."*

If you are working very hard while noticing that someone else is getting the recognition, you may be dealing with a "protected person." Avoid the temptation to level the playing field. ·

A protected person is the person that a supervisor (usually your superior) thinks can do no wrong. You will not convince the protector of any flaws. There are various reasons why the person is protected. It may be beauty, youth, friendliness or skill, but mostly it is because the person makes the protector feel important or preserves the protector's job in some way. To succeed in any establishment, it is important to find out who the protected ones are.

When I worked for the government, there were major changes in some of the processes, and a task force was created to make smooth transition to an electronic document management system. The task force consisted of three protected women who were unfamiliar with the business model, but were given staff to help implement the project. While the protected ones sat and talked for hours or read magazines, the staff did their work and never got any recognition. Nobody said anything.

Later, I was selected to train the protected ones along with other employees, and I decided to make a change. It was clear that these three women supported each other's lax management styles. So when I developed the training schedule, I deliberately placed them in separate training sessions.

When they received the training schedule, they went directly to my supervisor to complain. They didn't come to me because protected people do not deal with peers or those that they consider beneath them.

Keep in mind that protected people may be in their positions because they make themselves the sole conduit to management. The fact that everyone believes that they are the way to reach management gives them the ability to rule their domain.

I was summoned to my supervisor's office and told to change the schedule to put these women in the same class. Smiling, I told him that I could not do that because the schedule was already distributed. He offered to talk to the other managers and rearrange the rosters so that these women could be in the same class.

Being determined, soon I was working diligently to convince the other managers not to rearrange their staffs' schedules. But I made a mistake. I scheduled the most contentious protected woman for the last class, knowing that she would be the hardest to deal with. Also, I knew that making her last would infuriate her.

When the training began, the protected women consistently disagreed with my interpretations of the training manual and tried to monopolize the classes. Finally, on the last day of training, I had enough and asked the protected one in the class why, if she was so smart, she wasn't the instructor.

It is important to keep in mind our own attitudes in dealing with protected people. We always must be sure of where our feelings lie. A dislike for anyone because of their preferred position will always be reflected in your actions and cause you problems.

Later that day I stopped by my supervisor's office to let him know how the training had gone. But as I got there, the protected woman that I had rebuffed was leaving his office. I was about to tell him that she had caused problems during the training, but when I mentioned her name, he exploded. I was not prepared for his verbal assault. He accused me of jealousy and bad behavior, and for the remainder of my employment under him, he considered me a troublemaker and I could never do anything right. He saw my treatment of the protected one as an attack on himself.

I have also worked under supervisors who were themselves protected ones. In one case, my supervisor was a very friendly person but with no experience in her field. As a result, she depended on her staff to make decisions that she should have made and even relied on me to write her annual evaluations. Soon, her staff was performing all of her responsibilities and taking on projects that she was given. If you complained, she accused you of not being a team player and it was reflected in your annual evaluation.

Once when she was on leave and I was acting in her place, her boss asked me, "Why are you not supportive of your supervisor? She is your manager, and you should assist her any way you can." Defending myself, I answered, "I've helped her ever since she has been here. I even do things she should be doing."

"She is your manager. So do what she says," he continued.

"Okay, I'll do that," I said.

I began doing her managerial job, such as monitoring her staff hour usage monthly, and giving her the results. Knowing that she did not understand how staff hours were figured, I tried to teach her how to do it and why it was important. She was not interested in learning and, as a results, she used staff hours as if there were no limit. When I informed her that she was using too many staff hours, even sending her a memorandum, it was ignored.

Staff hours were burgeoning. I let it go, but was concerned.

Some time later, her supervisor summoned me to his office and asked why I didn't keep my manager informed of staff time usage. He didn't believe that I told her of my concerns several times. In my frustration, I mistook the conversation as an opportunity to tell him about my supervisor's laziness and the discontent she fueled in the staff.

Too late, I saw his anger, which was directed at me. He said, "Why should I believe you over your supervisor? She has no reason to lie to me."

I became so angry my words tumbled over each other as I said, "I have a memorandum that I sent showing that she was using too many staff hours and offering suggestions to correct the problem. I will go get the memo to show you."

But it didn't matter. The only thing that mattered was that I had suggested to him that she was imperfect. Even with the memorandum, his anger never abated.

Your life will be happier if you avoid any contact with the protected one. Unless you are ready to make a tough decision that will affect your career, under no circumstances complain to the sponsor about the protected one. If you do, you will be the bad guy and will cause the sponsor to be even more protective. The protector may even turn on you.

If you must have contact with the protected one, avoid any reference to the sponsor. Likewise, only mention the name of the protected one to the sponsor if the sponsor brings up the protected one's name, and then select your words very carefully and noncommittally.

One successful approach when the sponsor wants to talk to you about the protected one may be to repeat to the sponsor only what the sponsor has said about the protected one. For example:

Sponsor: "That Suzie Q. is really something!"

You: "You said it!"

Sponsor: "Suzie Q. is handling the XYZ account skillfully, and I hope that she's getting everyone's support."

You: "I'm glad that things are working out as you hoped."

Sponsor: "How can Suzie Q. be a better manager?"

You: "Now, that's an interesting question! Maybe that is a question you should ask her."

Let's be honest. We all want to be the protected one. Wisdom demands that we check our true feelings towards protected ones to make sure that we are not making our situation worse through jealousy, envy or frustration.

If you are the protected person, be grateful, and remember the Christian graces. It is always in poor taste (and not very smart) to make life miserable for anyone you work with. Remember the old adage that goes, "Be careful how you treat people as you climb up the ladder of success because you may meet the same people on your way down."

— CHAPTER 11 —

PICK YOUR BATTLES

Rule: Every battle is not worth fighting. If you fight every little battle, not only will you exhaust yourself and get the reputation of being argumentative, you will not be taken seriously when a real war erupts.

There are many battles, large and small, in a war. An insignificant battle is one that will cause you little harm or distress regardless of the outcome. If left alone, most of these skirmishes eventually go away on their own.

Know when to fight a battle and when to leave it for another day. For example, once when I asked my manager to let me work on a special project, she refused. At that time I did not ask her why or cause a fuss because I knew that it was not the right time for that battle.

Several months later, I approached her again. Her ambiguous response let me know that it was time for battle. So I threatened to go to her supervisor if she could not giving me a good reason for refusing my request. Going to her supervisor was as act of insubordination, and my threat evoked an immediate reaction from my manager. I considered this was a battle worth fighting because my career goal was at stake.

The next day, my manager called me to her desk and told me that I was selected to be an instructor.

Don't start a battle unless you are sure you can win. Sometimes it is best to simply ignore the individual who approaches you intending to do battle unless his behavior is so egregious that it will cause you harm if you don't engage in the fight.

Such was the case with one newly appointed manager. She was not qualified for her job and relied on her staff to perform her managerial duties. As a result, she was insecure in her staff and in her position.

Soon, she began segregating staff, and staff meetings were scenes of public humiliation for some staff members.

At our meetings, she accused me of undermining her because I wanted her position.

I did not defend myself because talking to her would make it worse. I also knew that a war had started in which there would be many battles. Nevertheless, I began to plan my battle strategy. Using her paranoia, I started smiling more than usual in our meetings, taking copious notes and timing my participation in meetings unless directly addressed.

One time her fears worked against her and became evident to senior management. My strategy was to let her hang herself through my meekness. When she accused me to co-workers or management, I let my work record and relationship with peers speak for me.

One day after I had been on leave, her supervisor called me into his office. He was usually friendly, but when I entered he looked out of the window with his back to me. Without turning around, he said, "Your manager is being removed; I need a position to put her on."

When he turned around and saw my face, he looked surprised and said, "I thought the director had talked to you about it. I'm sorry, I thought you knew."

She was transferred the next week to a very undesirable position without employees or secretary. There had been a lot of battles, but I had won the war.

There are people who like battles. But sometimes it is more satisfying not to be goaded into a battle and watch a one-sided battle fizzle out.

In college, my friend seemed to be energized by battles, and everything was a cause for a fight to her. She liked a special type of toothpaste. One day I reached into the medicine cabinet and seized the first tube of tooth paste my hand found, but it happened to be the type that she liked. When she saw me using it, she was livid, ran up to me and asked why I had taken her toothpaste. I turned and with a smile handed her the tube, apologizing. It was most gratifying to see the air go out of her sails.

I don't like battles and I sure don't like a war, so I will go out of my way to avoid them. I have found that there are certain actions and words that trigger battles. One of the words is "you." The word "you" has an accusative tone and will gender immediate anger.

For example, I was working with co-workers on a project that was vitally important to my annual evaluation. I wanted to discuss the timeliness of the project because the deadline was quickly approaching. We called a meeting, and I said to the project manager, "Now we will miss the deadline because 'you' didn't keep us informed of the time frame." She got irate because I had accused her of failing to do her job.

It would have been better had I said, "I'm afraid that we will miss the deadline now." Changing my statement would have eliminated the accusative tone and focused on the project instead of the project manager.

In another example, an employee was clearly frustrated about procedures she didn't understand and attacked me verbally, saying, "You gave me a project that you knew I couldn't handle. Are you setting me up?" I said, "I don't understand the problem. Help me see what is wrong." Responding this way took the employee out of the attack mode. I involved myself in her problem and redirected her energy back to the problem instead of our personalities. Nonetheless, a better approach for her in addressing me may have been to say, "I need help with the project I've been assigned. Can you help me?"

Almost always, defusing the emotions or redirecting the subject is wiser and more productive than waging all-out war.

— CHAPTER 12 —

BE ANGRY AND SIN NOT

Rule: Being angry makes you do stupid things. Everybody gets angry sometimes.

The question is, how do you handle your anger? "Be angry and sin not" *(Ephesians 4:26)*. This is Biblical instruction, but it's also the very best anger management advice that anyone could give you. It means don't let people dictate your feelings by pushing your buttons to make you say things that you will regret later.

Silence is the first line of defense. All of us have "hot buttons," but don't let people know what they are or they will forever be pushing one or two just to see you jump. But to do this, you must first know what your hot buttons are. Learn those parts of your own personality that are sensitive so that you will recognize when you are prone to over react and harden yourself. If, by accident or intentionally, someone pushes one of your hot buttons, don't let that person know it, even if you must bite your tongue so hard that you taste the blood to do so. Your facial expression must not give you away, so practice your poker face.

Sometimes you should show your anger and frustration, but be sure that you do it at the appropriate time and place and for the right reason, and always keep your anger under control. If it is an ongoing situation that is causing you anger, whether with your employer or your peer, control your feelings and, when you are completely calm, confront it. But don't let it boil too long.

Boiling may result in your not being able to control yourself and suddenly exploding. When that happens, your anger may be labeled moodiness and lack of self-control. When you explode, your anger controls and you lose all perspective. Don't let them see you sweat, never completely lose it.

With every ugly situation, you can practice controlling your anger and get better at doing it. This is a maturing process. Here is a description of one time that I boiled.

I was given an assignment to train hundreds of employees. One of my manager's favorite fair-haired women was in the class. She had never liked me, and frankly, the feeling was mutual.

She found fault with everything that went on in the class. First, the co-instructors talked too loudly. Then I talked too softly or we did not present the training material in an understandable way or breaks were not given often enough.

Finally, my patience fled and I told her to be quiet or leave the classroom. She decided to remain in class, but with an attitude that disturbed the entire class. When class was over, she furiously left the room. Something in the back of my mind said, "You are in for it now," but I ignored it.

After class, my manager summoned me into his office. Thinking that he would congratulate me for a job well done, I was taken aback when I saw his livid face.

When he asked why I had embarrassed his favorite manager, I saw red. He did not give me the opportunity to tell him what had happened, but assumed that I was the troublemaker.

I completely lost it. I cried, shook, yelled, the whole bit. By the time I left his office, I was embarrassed, hurt and humiliated, mostly because other employees had seen and heard my explosion. It took a long time to live it down.

Never argue with your manager no matter how angry he has made you or how out of control he may be. If you are in a meeting, just state your position on the issue and leave it at that. No matter how nicely you say it, your boss will get angry if you continue to debate an issue, especially if he has closed the door on the subject. You may feel like you are going to explode unless you say what is on your mind, but bite your tongue hard.

Remember, "everything that comes up don't have to come out." Know when to take a stand and when to back down, even if you are positive that you are right about an issue.

Learn to ignore things that are not relevant; discussing them will only lead to discussions that will not be beneficial to either of you.

Getting into a shouting match with anyone is not wise. There is an old saying that, "If someone is passing by, she will not know which one is the fool."

Keep your sense of humor. If you feel that you just must say something or explode, say under your breath without anyone hearing you and with a smile on your face, "You are a jerk and will always be a jerk. So why do I think you will change?" That always gave me a sense of satisfaction.

— CHAPTER 13 —

DON'T SPILL YOUR GUTS

Rule: There are things on the inside of you that should stay there. Everything that comes up should not come out.

Keeping confidences will take you far in any organization and give you favor with your manager, peers and employees. They know that whatever they tell you will not become water-cooler gossip or be used against them in the future.

Some people like to talk just to hear their head rattle. The Bible says, "A fool's voice is known by his multitude of words" *(Ecclesiastes 5:3).* Putting it another way, don't talk just to be talking or trying to impress your listeners. If you do in a work-related situation, you will be labeled a tattle-tale, know-it-all or show-off. People who talk too much eventually end up telling something they were told in confidence. Also, it's annoying to listen to someone who can't stay on the topic at hand.

Share your knowledge with others when asked, but don't volunteer answers when they are not directed to you. Volunteering information will make others think that you are acting superior to them, and they will resent you. Confidentially, there are times when you make yourself indispensable by not sharing information, especially when it is not asked for. Being the only one capable of performing a job lends to your indispensability.

Never give a person enough rope to hang you. The way Momma put it was, "Don't spill your guts." What she meant was that there is a time to keep your mouth shut and speak only when you are spoken to. I am not saying to be dishonest, but if the information is a key that you use for yourself alone and does not damage or harm others, then keep it to yourself. If you are not asked, don't volunteer. This might be just the leverage that will give you the advantage in the future.

There are things that you should not tell even your closest friend about yourself or others, personal things that could affect yourself or others. *(Please refer to Chapter 8, "Play with a Puppy and It Will Lick Your Mouth.")* Even in performing your job, there are times when you don't tell your co-workers about all of the processes or tools that you have developed for your own personal use. This is not being selfish; it is making life easier for you. Of course, if the processes or tools will benefit your organization, it should be shared.

There have been many times when I have given others what I thought was additional helpful information to my detriment. Once, when a co-worker asked me a question on a regulation, I not only gave him the information he requested, but went on to give him other interpretations and opinions and how these facts related to side issues he may have been interested in. One or two minutes into my explanation, I sensed that something was wrong. Looking at him, I saw that he was angry. Surprised, I stopped my dialogue and asked him if there was anything else he needed. He told me that I had done too much and that he was back at square one. In other words, I have confused him by spilling my guts. He left unappreciative and thinking that I was showing off to make him feel dumb.

On one job, my manager asked me to provide her with information that it was her responsibility to maintain, but for my own satisfaction I had started my file, too. When my manager's supervisor asked her for the information, she had inadvertently misplaced her copy. My manager lied and told her manager that I had not given her the information. Fortunately, I had kept a copy along with the transmittal letter I sent to her and gave it to her supervisor.

It is always advisable to cover yourself, so keep notes, letters, e-mail or any documentation that you feel might be necessary should you need to vindicate yourself or prove your actions in situations that might become adversarial or controversial.

Learn all you can, not only about your assigned area but other areas, and never refuse a detail or work project from another program area.

Remember that knowledge is power, so don't give your power away easily. Practice discretion. Give others information as they ask for it, and only give them the information specifically asked for.

— CHAPTER 14 —

REPEATING YOURSELF
CAN BE A GOOD THING

Rule: *Nobody likes to repeat herself for fear of being called stupid, but at times, repeating things makes your life easier. At times, it can even be a lifesaver. Mirroring, a way of repeating yourself, is an effective tool to make sure that you and your manager understand what is required.*

Repeating yourself can be especially helpful if you are an instructor. But how you repeat yourself depends on your students.

In preparing for my first training job I had been told to watch the students' faces to determine whether they understood what I was relating. The class I taught was technical, so with almost every sentence I asked the class if they understood the concept. Sometimes they looked at me with blank expressions, and when this happened, I restated the concept using other words. Finally, I saw understanding flash in some of their eyes. That gave me great pleasure, but I did not consider that people have different levels of understanding. I continued to repeat myself, but then one of the students said, "Do you think we are stupid? Why are you repeating the same thing over and over?"

At break, another student came to me in tears saying, "I still don't get it! Just because she understood it doesn't mean we all understand it. So will you go over it again?"

After break, I paired the students who had gotten the concept with those who had not understood. It worked beautifully, for all of the students and I had learned a good lesson. Repeating is good, but knowing your audience tells you when to stop.

Now there is a right way and a wrong way to repeat yourself.

Some people feel that it is somehow demeaning to have to repeat themselves. I never understood why, so I asked somebody once and her response was, "They should be listening."

If you don't like repeating yourself, consider using the "mirroring" technique. Ask your listener to repeat back to you what you just said. Mirroring is a tool that can be very helpful in situations where you want to be sure your instructions are clearly understood or you want to make sure that you understand what you're told.

For instance, to be sure that you understand what your boss is saying, ask him/her to repeat the instructions. If she/he is one of those bosses who do not like to repeat herself/himself, parrot what you heard her/him say. This will invite her/him to correct any misunderstanding. To mirror someone, start your sentence with phrases like: "I understand that you are saying . . .," or, "So you want me to ..." or, "Do you mean..."

Another technique is rephrasing. This is when you say the same thing over again but in a different way. The thought is, if you say it several ways, the person you are talking to has several opportunities to understand it. For instance, you can tell your boss, "I will be on vacation next week, but I've finished the project you gave me." Later in the day, you can tell your boss, "When you pick up the project on my desk next week, I will make any changes you want when I get back from vacation."

Use the technique that works best for you, but the point is understanding exactly what is being said.

— CHAPTER 15 —

LEARN TO LISTEN

Rule: A good listener will be liked and can go far in any organization, but good listeners are as rare as trained alley cats.

Everybody wants to talk, but nobody wants to listen. You can see it on television, hear it on the radio and observe it with friends and family. People especially don't want to hear about your personal problems, but are more than willing to pile their personal problems on you.

Few people are born with the skill of listening. It is an art that most people must develop.

Being a good listener means shutting your mouth and really paying attention to what someone is saying. It also means letting the other person know you are listening by eye contact and an occasional nod or grunt. Don't let your mind wander.

Sometimes people just need to talk. Talking it out makes things seem clearer, gives the person another perspective or helps the person make a decision she would not have otherwise made. She is often not seeking advice or counsel but just a listening ear.

Listening shows that you value other's concerns, ideas and feelings. It shows that you care about them to the point of spending time with them.

Once I was tutoring a young girl who was so fidgety and distracted that she could not learn. In frustration, I told her to "listen!" She looked at me with surprise, and I realized that she had no idea what I meant. I composed myself and told her to be quiet, sit still and focus her eyes on me. It worked like a charm and she learned quickly thereafter.

I thought I was a good listener until one of my daughters told me, "Momma, you don't let people finish their sentences before you jump in." She was right! This was not only rude, but resulted in my not hearing what she was really trying to make me understand. In my eager-ness to help understand her, I was not letting her finish her sentences. Learning to listen to my daughters since then has not only made for richer relationships with them but some surprising revelations!

There is another more subtle benefit to being a good listener. Cul-tivating the art of listening and being able to keep a confidence will result in your getting first-hand information on things that others don't know. For example, if a co-worker tells you she is transferring or leav-ing, you can have your resume ready and be the first to apply for the position. You can be among the first to know information on company reorganizations that may affect your position. You may also start to understand that person who you thought did not like you or who you did not like.

Keep in mind that being a good listener does not mean you be-coming a garbage dump. Turn off people talking about your manager or peers. My mother used to say, "Anyone who talks to you about a person will talk about you!" Stay clear of her!

Remember, information is power, but gossip is trouble.

— CHAPTER 16 —

GO TO THE SOURCE

Rule: The majority of misunderstandings can be avoided if you know the source of their origin before taking action. Before acting, "Go to the horse's mouth."

Never believe rumors about your manager or co-workers. It is not always easy or possible to get to the root of a rumor, but it is essential that you try to do so before acting or believing it.

If more than one person is involved, don't talk to them individually. Confront them together. Talking with them separately will get you nowhere because they will have separate stories that are subjective and that may be very different.

Be forthright in your conversations. If you are having a problem with a co-worker who has gone to your supervisor to accuse you and returned with orders for you from your supervisor, before believing your co-worker, ask your supervisor to meet with both of you. It will not be easy to get all of you together, but it will be worth it. That way, your supervisor will have both sides of the story, draw her own conclusions, and you will hear yourself what you are to do.

E-mail is an excellent tool to use in cases where there is a controversy with you stuck in the middle. Example: You are co-chair on a project, and all members of the group are assigned a part of the project to be completed by an established deadline. E-mail is a good way to stay in direct contact with each project member without the status of third-party relays.

Perhaps you have discussed an important deadline with your co-chair, but she just doesn't seem to get it or care a hoot about deadlines or what your manager wants.

E-mail to the chairperson, with copies to her and your managers addressing the problem, will work wonders. Be sure to include all of the facts in the e-mail, including your concern that the deadline will not be met. However, never point fingers or place blame. Merely address your concerns and ask for the uncooperative co-chair to give guidance on how she recommends that the project proceed in light of the time line.

You are not trying to get the chairperson in hot water, you are just trying to let her and your managers know the project situation. Conversely, the co-chair will get the point of how important you consider it is to complete the project in a timely manner. She may even respect that you are not going behind her back to your manager.

— CHAPTER 17 —

TAKE EVERYTHING YOU CAN,
BUT DON'T CAN EVERYTHING YOU TAKE

Rule: *After Momma gathered fruits and vegetables for canning, she carefully picked out the debris, stems and old leaves and said, "I take everything I can, but I don't can everything I take."*

The farm I was raised on was self-sufficient. We produced all of our meats, vegetables and fruits, and I watched Momma can almost everything. We grew peanuts, corn and sorghum. The only things we bought from the store were sugar, salt, black pepper, flour and flavorings.

It seemed that every year swarms of honey bees stopped in our trees, and Dad made hives for them. When the bees made honey in the hives, Dad made a wire mesh for his head, donned pants and tied them at the bottom around his legs, put on gloves, and robbed the hives of honey. Soon after that, the bees would leave for other destinations.

Momma started her canning in late summer and continued until fall or until all of the crops were gathered. We were constantly washing jars and lids and hearing pops in the night as the jars sealed.

As Momma picked debris from the fruits and vegetables she wanted to can, sometimes she removed what was called "milkweeds," which could hardly be distinguished from the real greens. As I closely watched Momma, I asked her why was she threw away seemingly good stuff. She showed me what she was throwing away and said, "You gather everything. Some of it is good to eat and some of it is not good to eat. Some will upset your stomach, some will give you a headache, and some can even kill you. Milkweed looks exactly like mustard greens, but it will make you sick."

I asked Momma, "Then, why gather the parts that can't be canned?" She explained, "Sometimes the parts that cannot be canned serve a purpose. When I pull corn off of the stalks, I don't take the shucks right off because it keeps the corn fresh until I get ready to can it. Just like when I pull up the turnip greens, I keep the greens on the turnips until I am ready to can the greens. But look at the stems of the mustard greens. I do not can them because they are tuff and bitter, but they help preserve the greens until I am ready to can them."

Momma's advice is good for life in general. When listening to people, whether family, acquaintances, co-workers or the media, listen to everything being said, but filter out those things that are untrue or are inapplicable.

In the workplace, rumors will fly and everyone will have their opinions about what is going on or how to run things. Listen to what the people around you say, but don't feel obligated to take what they say as the reality of the situation.

A friend told me that she was applying for a position that was rumored to become vacant because the incumbent was being fired. She suggested that I also apply, so I did that very day. When my application got to Personnel, they sent it back via my manager, asking where did I get the information, because there was no vacancy. I had listened to a rumor that had no merit.

Sometimes people are upset because I listen to what they have to say but do not put their ideas of advice into action. But if you are wise, you will carefully select what becomes a part of your life.

— CHAPTER 18 —

DON'T CLOSE ANY DOORS

Rule: When leaving one position for another, be sure that you leave under favorable conditions because the future is unpredictable.

Momma told me a story about a man who was being pursued by a group of men trying to do him bodily harm. As he ran, he came to a river and quickly crossed the bridge. His pursuers were gaining ground behind him, so he decided to burn the bridge he had just crossed so that they could not follow him.

After burning the bridge, he came face to face with another group more furious than the one behind him. Now he was in a real dilemma! He could not go back because he had burned the bridge behind him. So he was killed because of his lack of foresight.

The same analogy applies to closing doors behind you in the work place. What does it mean to close a door behind you? It means leaving with feelings of animosity between you and your boss, co-workers or employees because you think you will never have to deal with them again.

Always leave the door open. You may want to come back through it.

For example, a clerk who worked in my area applied for and got a job at another agency. I didn't blame her because the other job paid more and had more opportunities for promotion. She was a good employee with an ever-pleasing attitude, so she left with my blessings. At that time I did not know that she had previously worked for my manager.

A month later, she called asking for her job back. Because her old position was not yet filled, I asked my boss to reinstate her. I was astonished when he refused. He said that because she left on her own and when we needed her, he would not rehire her.

After much discussion, he finally allowed her to return. I was willing to stand on her behalf because she did not leave me with a bad taste in my mouth or burned her bridge.

On the other hand, another one of my staff applied for a job elsewhere. He was an excellent writer, and I learned to rely on him for special writing assignments. But he had a bad attitude that showed in staff meetings and in his dealings with staff members. As he left, everyone was glad and he made no bones about stating his relief to be gone.

At the last minute, the agency where he had applied changed its plans because of a hiring freeze. He asked me for his job back.

Even though his expertise was an asset, he was a troublemaker. I needed someone who would bring unity to the group, so I did not take him back. He had closed the door behind him.

Along the same line, one of my co-workers decided to leave her job to work for a family business. However, she was bitter. As she left, she threw recriminations at all present and flung all of her pent-up venom at her employer, loudly and in the presence of professional and administrative staff. The door was firmly closed on her ever returning, should her family business fold, or holding a relationship with her co-workers.

I had always wanted to be a school teacher, but never succeeded in that goal. At one of my jobs, an announcement was made that instructors were needed, and I was very familiar with the procedures that would be taught. I asked my manager to submit my name to the Training Department. I was informed the next day that I would not be selected for training because the lead instructors did not want me to serve with them. In fact, they said that they would quit if I were selected, and they said some awfully nasty things about me.

A few months later the announcement was again made for new instructors. I again asked my manager to submit my name. This time the agency was so desperate for instructors that they accepted me. The lead instructors were so angry that they refused to teach, and I became the lead instructor.

Several months later, one of the instructors went to another agency. I thought I would never hear from him again, but several years later he wanted to come back to the agency and gave my name as a reference which was a major mistake. He never came back to work at the agency because he had badly burned his bridges behind him.

When I was discouraged on my job and considered quitting, a close friend once told me never to leave a job on the downswing. Always leave when everything is going well; that way, you know that you probably aren't burning too many bridges behind you, and you leave with your reputation intact. Remembering these words has kept me from making rash employment decisions.

Rash or quick decisions often backfire. "Sow in haste, reap at leisure." "Think before you leap." "The grass is not always greener on the other side of the fence."

When climbing the ladder of success, never mistreat other workers in your advancement, and keep these old sayings in mind. "You may meet the same ones on your way up that you will meet on your way down."

THE WOMAN MANAGER
AND ENTREPRENEUR

There is a difference between male and female managers, and women bosses seem to have a bad reputation. Most of the people I know, especially women, say that they prefer male bosses to female. However, the November 2003 *Readers' Digest* said, "Seventy-six percent of us would be comfortable having a female president." How strange!

More women are becoming entrepreneurs, corporate executives and business owners. Therefore, many find themselves in positions of authority that are new to them, and they may feel pressured to exceed the standards set by their male counterparts, and there is the tendency to go too far to show that they are as good as the guys. Still, they may also fear being perceived as pushy, bossy or emotional.

I have noted in my management career that male managers have the ability to be personal friends, but easily resume their roles as managers during working hours. They go fishing, golfing, hunting, to ball games or just out for an afternoon of fun with their male staff, but at the office retain business decorum.

However, even in these modern days, a female manager must be more careful in the work environment than her male counterpart.

This does not seem to be the case for female managers. Often, if a female manager is sociable, especially with her female employees, thereafter they are not given respect on the job. If the female manager acts sociably with a male employee, she may be accused of wanting to have an affair with him.

As a manager for thirty years, I found that there are certain things that just don't work for female managers.

I don't understand the dynamics of male relationships in the office. But, as a female manager, you need to understand that friendships with your staff can turn quickly to disrespect, especially during yearly evaluations when you must grade their work habits. It is very awkward explaining to your "friend" why you are giving her a less than favorable evaluation. Because you are friends, a female employee may feel that you should give her a good rating regardless of how poor her performance was. Because you are friends, you may have neglected to give her the regular performance feedback she needed. To worsen the situation, there will be the tendency to rate your friend harder so that other employees will not accuse you of favoritism.

Female managers do seem more prone, in my experience, to act more favorably toward those with personalities they like. This adds to the prejudice against business women, because they are perceived as unfair. There will inevitably be employees who work harder and try harder to be the very best. You may not like the attitude or personality of the employee, but her evaluation should always stand on her work record, not your like or dislike of her.

Favoritism is unacceptable in any situation. Don't do more for one employee or act differently toward an employee because that person is or is not your favorite. You must keep it on a professional level. To prevent unnecessary trouble, just keep professional relationships separate from personal relationships.

Equal and consistent application of rules and regulations is a must. My supervisor assigned a project to another manager and me to work together. The project was major and would impact all of the departments in the agency. We worked well together and the project was completed ahead of schedule, and the results were of high quality.

As a result, we were both given performance awards. I received $300, but later discovered that my co-worker was given $500. When I asked my supervisor why my co-worker got $200 more then I did, at first she said that awards were confidential and asked who told me the amount of my co-worker's award.

When I refused to divulge the source, she got angry and said, "I can give an award in amount I want to. What are you complaining about? You got an award as well."

I knew that awards were given at the supervisor's discretion, but there were guidelines stating that project leaders working in tandem were to receive the same award amount. I also knew that my co-worker and the manager were good friends. I said nothing further, but I was hurt and disappointed by the inconsistent treatment. I promised myself that I would be consistent in dealing with my employees.

Acknowledge and defeat your own demons before trying to manage the demons of others. It is good to be self-confident, but it is a mistake to think you have all of the answers just because you are the boss.

One demon even the best boss must overcome is the reluctance to delegate. Too much hands-on supervision shows that you lack confidence in your staff's ability.

I was always overwhelmed with work. My desk was piled so high that I could hardly find space to work, and it seemed that I was always behind in my work though I came in early, stayed late, and took work home on the weekends. I knew that I was in trouble when I missed a critical deadline.

One day, a friend, who had been a manager for years, looked at my desk and said, "You have too much hands-on. Trust your employees to do a good job and they just might surprise you."

It wasn't easy to turn loose at first. Finally, I forced myself just to review the work my staff did and release it without hovering and nitpicking, and I was pleasantly surprised to see the change in my staff. They became more self-confident, didn't come to me with as many questions, and learned to keep me informed only if problems arose. The pile of work on my desk soon disappeared, and I was able to attend to the administrative chores necessary for managers, which had been consistently late before.

Another personal demon of the woman supervisor or employer is failing to confront problems in a timely manner. For the sake of maintaining relationships, we tend to let resentment boil and fume until it explodes. Then we hit the offender with everything that has piled up inside — even issues that should have been confronted months ago.

Failure to confront problems as they arise will lose time and energy later. At times, when I did not want to confront the offender, I called a meeting with the entire staff to discuss the issue as though it involved them all. One day after such a meeting, another employee asked why I had called a meeting for the entire staff when the problem was with just one employee. I hadn't realized that it was so obvious and grudgingly acknowledged to the employee that he was right. After that, I no longer called staff meetings just to reprimand one individual.

There are times when the issue should not be addressed immediately, usually when you are so angry that anything you say will be unprofessional. In such situations, give yourself time to cool down, but not so much time that the incident is no longer fresh in the mind of the employee.

If you are fortunate enough to have your own business, the same rules apply. Don't have favorites. Resist the urge to try to be friends with your employees and apply all rules equally.

There is one more problem that you will confront as a female business owner. Don't expect your employees to match your dedication to the company. They are there for the paycheck, but you have your life's blood, savings and future tied to the business. It is your "baby," not theirs. So get over the idea that telling them something once is enough or that they will give it all they have, fast. Always be prepared to repeat your instructions as many times as necessary — but not forever. If an employee doesn't get it after telling her a few times, don't waste more time on her. But if an employee is making even slow progress, consider keeping her on.

My mother's advice to take everything you can but don't can everything you take also applies here. No one is perfect. If your employee's benefits outweigh his detriments, learn to cultivate those benefits and try to mentally discard the detriments. If the employee is not performing his job at an acceptable level, don't hesitate to counsel him or even dismiss him. The quicker the better. Don't let him get in the habit of doing it incorrectly.

Nevertheless, even though the business is yours, you must trust your employees to do their jobs. You will be constantly bogged down with clerical and even technical work if you are too much hands-on.

A manager or business owner should always maintain a professional work environment. I asked a professional woman who had recently quit her position at a major government agency, just why had she resigned. The pay was good, the hours of work were acceptable, and the benefits were the best. She said, "I just couldn't tolerate the unprofessionalism in the office. The shouting from one cubicle to another, while some slept at their desks. Little work was done and that which was done was incomplete and inaccurate. But what troubled me more than anything was that the supervisor knew about those conditions and did nothing to correct them and could not because he was as bad as they were."

Don't second-guess yourself. It's better to make a well-considered guess than sit on the fence indefinitely. Your staff will sense it if you're wishy-washy, and they will become resentful and defensive. They will lose all respect for you if you appear to be unable to run your own ship.

As the woman in charge, you set the tone for everyone else's behavior, attitude and productivity. They look to you for cues. You can't and shouldn't expect your staff to have more integrity and dedication than you do. With some "mother wit," you can do it!

OTHER BOOKS BY ICY D GINES

God Don't Make Oops! — *$19.95*

Icy D Gines was born with ectrodactyly, a congenital disorder that left her with one finger on each hand and one toe on each foot, during a time when a physically challenged child was considered a disgrace to the family and hidden from view.

This 500-page autobiography chronicles her struggles, failed relationships, and business entanglements.

From the beginning, she had three strikes against her — she was handicapped, black and female. She could scarcely afford another strike if she was going to make it!

Her life of triumphs and disappointments made her conclude that, regardless of the package a life comes wrapped in, it is still a gift of infinite possibilities … the God who created every form of life doesn't make "OOPS"!

To order a copy of *God Don't Make Oops!,* please contact:

Icy D Gines
P.O. Box 18717
Raytown, MO 64133
Phone: 816/358-8116
Fax: 816/358-9313